Oppositional Defiant Disorder

Oppositional Defiant Disorder

A Mother's Survival

Zenia Marsden

Plicata Press

Oppositional Defiant Disorder
A Mother's Survival

©2014 Zenia Marsden
ISBN: 978-0-9828205-8-2
LCCN: 2013937348

Cover including graphics by the author.

Printed in the USA on acid free paper.

Plicata Press
P.O. Box 32
Gig Harbor, WA 98335
www.plicatapress.com

For all the frustrated parents of Oppositional Defiant Disorder children trying to hang onto their sanity while struggling to cope with self-blame, guilt, and criticism by teachers, psychologists, and family members who can't begin to understand the depth and scope of the problem.

Acknowledgements

Special appreciation to: Colleen Slater, Frank Slater, Kristi Clark, Marjie Wood, Carolyn Willis, Susan Bettinger, Ted Olinger, and especially my editor Jan Walker.

To my son, who provided the background foundation for all the material in this true accounting of our lives before he matured into the wonderful man of whom I am so proud.

Foreword

A Special Ed Teacher says . . .

The biggest challenge in working with ODD kids is finding something positive that they will do to earn rewards and, conversely, establishing negative consequences they will try to avoid. What gets them to cooperate one day may not motivate them the next day. Teachers, who are bound by school policy, often exhaust their choices for rewards and disciplinary measures in a short time.

Another challenge is that many parents just give up on their ODD children. They expect the school to "fix" their kids; they don't follow up with positive and negative reinforcement at home.

I also work with kids who have Attention Deficit Hyperactivity Disorder (ADHD) Posttraumatic Stress Disorder (PTSD) bipolar diagnoses and some on the Autism Spectrum. ODD kids are by far the most disruptive in a learning environment. They are angry and frustrated, generally for unidentified reasons, and strike out verbally or physically, or both, when they're given directions or being corrected. **These children want total**

1

control. They become angry, defiant and destructive toward anyone who does not allow them to have that control.

Two paraprofessionals assist me in my classroom of 11 students. That's three more than the stated limit due to space and funding. We often stop focusing on academics to concentrate on dealing with disruptive behaviors. We have a quiet room where kids can go for short time out stays to calm down away from the rest of the class.

I run a tightly structured, consistent program, with many varied and short activities during the day, frequent breaks between activities, and immediate rewards and negative consequences for their behavior and academic achievement. They overlap. Following directions and completing assignments count as both proper behavior and academic progress.

We use a point system, in which points are earned for work completion and expected behaviors, and points are lost for lack of the same. Points are given and taken away consistently and immediately. My students relate to this system because it is objective, and it remains consistent.

ODD children are often suspended or expelled from schools where they're in regular classrooms. They are considered too time-consuming. They take a teacher's time and attention from children who function in the normal classroom setting. Society in general labels these children as "bad kids," without trying to understand then.

I enjoy working with them because they are smart, creative and interesting, and they deserve help to find their places in the world. They have the potential to become constructive contributing members of society. They need consistent reinforcement to learn trust and develop willingness to strive for their own positive outcomes. Each ODD child needs to be treated and taught as a unique individual. Each comes to school filled with anger, frustration and a sense of desperation at being unable to control their world.

Teaching these children has taught me patience and empathy. It has taught me to listen and observe, to look for what motivates them and triggers their reactions rather than expect them to conform to my demands as a classroom teacher.

Though behavioral scientists and therapists do not know how this disorder develops, they have established some guidelines for working with them. I earned a BA in general education and taught in regular elementary classrooms before earning an MA in psychology with residential experience at Western State Hospital Child Study and Treatment Center. I taught learning disabled children for four years, and have now taught Emotional/Behavioral Disordered children for 37 years.

Susan Bettinger, Special Education Teacher

Introduction

I didn't know ...

I didn't know why my son was so difficult. I struggled with his behavior for years. He was a challenge to teachers, frustrating to counselors, and a source of aggravation and guilt to his father and me.

I searched for answers and advice to help me understand my child and deal with undesirable behaviors that went far beyond the norm.

Unless you have experienced dealing with a child with Oppositional Defiance Disorder first-hand, it is impossible to comprehend the magnitude of difficulties that go along with the psychological diagnosis.

I decided to write about my experiences raising my son because I was aided in my own situation by talking to other parents who were faced with raising very difficult, strong-willed children. It is some comfort to know you are not alone. Other parents are out there dealing with ODD children. They don't share all the same problems, but they all struggle with children in a system that isn't equipped to deal with them adequately. If you think you have it bad, it helps to know others are struggling with children who have similar behaviors and are managing to get through it somehow. It is useful to learn alternative forms of discipline.

I feared for his life ...

My son caused me no end of grief. I feared for his future and his life. In spite of everything you will read in these pages, he turned out to be a decent, patriotic, law-abiding citizen. For many years I believed that was impossible.

Birth and Optimism

He was such a good baby ...

Jeremy was delivered by cesarean section. As the doctor lifted him out I studied his angelic face and nose, and large gray eyes. He was perfect, but I had severe obstetric complications that required bed rest for the first two months post-delivery.

My parents cared for Jeremy while my husband, Michael, worked 48 hour shifts as an emergency medicine physician. He would come home exhausted, and my parents would leave. He felt burned out by professional and family responsibilities while I continued struggling with recovery.

Jeremy was such a good baby, sleeping six hours straight from the very first night we brought him home. I was grateful to have such an easy-care baby. He gave us little trouble during those early months. He seldom cried, except when he was being dressed, which made him scream. Not cry, but scream at the top of his lungs; his face turning deep red as he wailed. Once dressed, his expression changed instantaneously to a smile.

1

Constantly in motion...

As weeks passed, Jeremy was constantly in motion. He didn't crawl yet, but he'd lie on his back, flailing his arms and legs as fast as he could. Bath-time, he sat in his plastic ring, sucking on a wet washcloth, pushing toys around in the water. He'd splash and laugh until it was time to get out unless it was time to wash his hair. Even years later, getting his hair shampooed sent him into fits of screaming rage but, when it was over, he didn't want to get out of the tub.

I wonder now if the flailing arms and legs were a sign of Jeremy's behavior issues.

Months flew by and before long he was crawling, slowly at first, but soon it was full speed ahead. Jeremy started to get into things. Anything within reach was fair game. He made the transition to walking by hanging onto furniture and pulling himself along. Then he walked without aids, looking for more things to get into.

We installed a child-proof gate between the living-room and kitchen to keep him out of the cupboards and to prevent him from going outside unattended. He was a busy, active child, just like any other toddler his age. We still had no inkling of what the future held.

A second gate...

One morning, while my husband was away on his long shift, I went downstairs to disaster. It was obvious Jeremy had been there during the night. All the cupboard doors were open, rice strewn in cabinets, on countertops and all over the indoor-outdoor carpet. That would have been

2

bad enough, but the spray-nozzle at the kitchen sink had been used to water down the whole room, including inside the cupboards. Sticky rice adhered to everything, and the carpet was soaked. I went back upstairs and Jeremy was asleep in his crib. There was no sign that he had been up creating havoc in the middle of the night. It took hours to clean the mess. The floor didn't dry out for days. I vowed never again to live in a house with a carpeted kitchen floor.

A second gate was added, above the first, to avert further catastrophic events. This was a successful deterrent. Other than typical spills and clutter, major messes were prevented.

We had two large dogs and three cats. Jeremy loved our pets and was gentle with them. The cats often snuggled with him on the sofa. The dogs remained close by whenever he went outside.

As Jeremy grew, he developed an increasing love of books. *Green Eggs and Ham* was a favorite, and he sat beside me on the sofa while I read the same worn pages over and over again. His own vocabulary was limited, but he was fascinated by the words and accompanying pictures.

I was exhausted ...

Michael was gone for days at a time, and had little time for our son, so looking after Jeremy was my responsibility. My parents lived a couple of hours away, but they babysat on occasion to give me a break.

Jeremy had endless energy and never walked if he could run. He drew on the walls with crayons, left toys everywhere and made messes wherever he went. The house was never clean and I was exhausted. I picked things up, mopped floors and scrubbed the walls, but Jeremy immediately spilled drinks and threw toys everywhere. I started cleaning house in the middle of the night so it would at least be clean until he got up in the morning.

When we went to family get-togethers, my mother repeatedly announced to everyone, "He's terrible two, he's terrible two," continuously apologizing for his errant behavior.

Still, this wasn't abnormal behavior for a toddler; intelligent and affectionate, we were quite sure our son was normal in every way. He very seldom cried. Our hopes were high.

Potty training...

All attempts at potty training failed dismally. Many people told me, "It often takes three years to potty train boys." I wasn't concerned.

I looked forward to Jeremy's third birthday—past terrible two and potty trained, changing diapers a thing of the past.

An energetic, busy, extraordinarily independent child, he was always smiling or laughing. We got a new small dog, a Pomeranian we named Chipper. Jeremy spent hours playing with the animals and loved carting Chipper around in his wagon when he wasn't getting into things in the house.

Construction of our new home began in September. Jeremy, the dogs, and I went out every weekday to watch the workers as our house took shape. The men were kind to him, and Jeremy observed the framers, electricians, plumbers and finish carpenters with fascination.

On one visit I'd left my purse and keys in the truck and found Jeremy had locked both doors. He loved to push the door-lock buttons. One of the workmen broke in through the back sliding window. Never again did I leave home without a spare key in my pocket.

New house ...

I worked in the yard and gardens at our home and planted new trees and shrubs in the grounds at our building site. Jeremy loved to rake the ground beside me or throw sticks for the dogs. It was a good time in our life.

We moved into our new house; our living space was now all on one level with a large unfinished basement downstairs. The halls, bathrooms, kitchen, family and dining rooms had vinyl floors; the rest of the house was carpeted, partitioned off with locked doors to keep pets and Jeremy confined to rooms that were easier to maintain. I expected to have more free time with the reduction of labor-intensive cleaning.

Jeremy's room was next to a bathroom and had a large window that looked out over the front entrance and garage. He had a walk-in closet and a new bed and dresser. The carpet was multicolored, mostly blues, but browns and reds and yellows. I thought it would hide stains well.

Third birthday ...

We celebrated his third birthday party a couple of months later. He was still wearing pull-ups, not yet potty-trained. "Terrible two" was over. I continued to remain optimistic, even though we were still struggling with the potty training issue. Jeremy's room was beginning to smell bad. He pointed to a place in his closet and said, "Kitty did it."

I cleaned up the mess and told him to keep the cat out of his room, but his room continued to stink. The closet had a very strong urine smell. I kept cleaning it up, but the odor continued to get stronger. I knew the cats weren't to blame, but it took a lot of questioning to get Jeremy to finally admit he'd done it.

He didn't mess his pants anymore, but I'd find human feces on the floor in his room, elsewhere in the house or on the ground outside. He urinated outside or on his floor rather than use the toilet. I kept cleaning up the messes, but couldn't get him to use the toilet in the bathroom. He started smearing feces on the walls and across the carpet. How I missed "the terrible twos" and messy diapers. I regretted having blue carpet installed. If I had known what the future held, I would have chosen mottled brown vinyl.

His behavior was unsanitary and frustrating. Nothing I did made any difference. Time-out wasn't working. Michael did little to help discipline our son. He was either away at work or continued to expect me to take care of the problem.

Isolated in the country ...

We lived isolated in the country. Jeremy was an only child and had no playmates. I frequently took him to visit families with children, but he did not interact well with them and he preferred to play alone.

My husband's forty-eight hour shifts kept him away from home much of the time. When he was home, he habitually stayed up at night and slept during the day. He didn't like to be disturbed when he was asleep and spent most of his waking hours at the computer.

Michael considered all yard, farm and housework my responsibility. He earned a living and expected me to do any and all other work associated with our home life, including providing Jeremy's care without his involvement. He remained far removed from participating in our son's upbringing.

I had little opportunity to take a break from my childrearing duties. Housecleaning was done in the middle of the night. At least things were clean until Jeremy woke up in the morning. There was a 24-hour grocery store six miles away, so I did our shopping alone in the wee hours of the morning on nights when Michael was home. Taking Jeremy to the store was very difficult and avoiding that provided me with brief periods of welcome escape.

Shopping with him was unpleasant most of the time. He never threw tantrums, but constantly grabbed things off the shelves and insisted I buy whatever he wanted. I seldom caved in to his demands, but it made shopping stressful. I preferred to go alone.

High expectations...

During the early years, our parents had high expectations for Jeremy. He was gregarious and outgoing in their presence and they doted on their young grandson who seemed to be the epitome of a child destined for success.

7

My own expectations were equally high. I had little experience with other children, so had no inkling that the majority of my issues were anything other than ordinary and certainly not abnormal. There was no doubt in my mind that Jeremy was a wonderful child. I dealt with the problems as well as I could and patiently looked forward to his maturing beyond the difficult behaviors, fully expecting these changes to occur in the not too distant future.

My mother-in-law informed me that the problem was me. After all, Jeremy behaved fine with everyone else.

Editor's Note:

The *Diagnostic and Statistical Manual of Mental Disorders, Fourth Edition* (DSM-IV) definition of Oppositional Defiant Disorder behaviors includes frequent temper tantrums and blaming others for mistakes or misbehavior.

An online review of the literature available on ODD symptoms suggests that there is a range between the normal behavior displayed during The Terrible Twos and behaviors of a child who has ODD.

The information states the behaviors do not occur only during the course of what might be diagnosed as a psychotic or mood disorder episode.

(See DSM IV & DSM IV-TR reference, page 88)

School

Montessori preschool, Age 4 ...

After he turned four, I enrolled Jeremy in a Montessori preschool run by a married couple. The school had a solid reputation for excellence and seemed to be a perfect opportunity for Jeremy to interact with a positive male role model, something he lacked at home given his dad's work hours and responsibilities. That fact helped guide my decision and made me optimistic.

Jeremy's dad and I had both loved school. We expected our young offspring to be equally enraptured with new experiences and making friends. I envisioned nothing less. My enthusiasm bubbled over as I explained to Jeremy how much fun he would have at school, meeting other children. He was, after all, a very bright child, and the concept of him hating school wasn't even on the radar.

He was nervous about going. When I dropped him off, he didn't want to go inside. I assured him it would just be for a short time. This was not unexpected. I was certain most parents faced similar circumstances on the first day.

Preschool sessions lasted two hours, too short a time for me to return home. It wasn't worth the hour-long round trip, so I went shopping. After four years of having him along or making my late night excursions to the store for quick purchases, his time at school allowed me to bask in the luxury of time alone. It seemed long overdue and I looked forward to the pleasant twice-a-week break.

I returned to pick up Jeremy and was met by his solemn, frowning face. When we got in the car he said, "I don't like school."

"Just wait. You'll change your mind." I believed he would and spoke in a pleasant and encouraging tone.

"No, I don't wanna go!" He hunched silently in his seat all the way home.

Every morning was a struggle ...

I was disturbed, but it had to be a minor, temporary situation. I couldn't imagine it continuing for an extended period of time. How could he not like school? I never even considered the possibility.

It became increasingly difficult to get him up in the morning. He did not want to go to school, and every morning was a struggle. As weeks went by, he developed a new tactic.

"I'm sick."

"What's wrong?" I was concerned.

"My tummy hurts."

"You can stay home today." I allowed him to remain in bed.

He made a miraculous recovery which made me suspicious. Normally a healthy child, he actually became sickly during that time. I attributed his health issues to exposure to other children and assorted germs. One morning when Michael was home, Jeremy was "sick" again. I woke Michael to check our son's symptoms and make a personal diagnosis. Having a doctor for a father doesn't work to the benefit of a child feigning illness.

Michael wasn't fooled, "You're not sick. You're going to school."

"No. I'm sick." Jeremy stiffened and clenched his fists. I got him dressed and took him to school.

It was much easier for him to convince me of ill health. I soon discovered that Jeremy became quite healthy whenever his dad was home. I had a preschooler already in the habit of skipping school. I stopped believing him. If he wasn't vomiting and didn't have a raised temperature, he went to school.

Trouble with simple rules ...

Conferences with his preschool teachers revealed puzzling and problematic behaviors. He wasn't fitting in well, and didn't get along with classmates. With the exception of using the bathroom properly at school, he was uncooperative and refused to follow simple rules or instructions. He didn't want to dress in blue jeans and tee shirts like the other kids in his class. Instead he insisted on wearing sweatpants and sweatshirts.

How could a very bright child who loved books and reading display such a total dislike of school? It was very disconcerting.

It was an unproductive year, both at school and at home. I was certain this had to be a temporary minor setback and that kindergarten in a standard public school the next year would turn things around.

It was becoming increasingly evident that the problems were not solely attributable to me, his mother and primary care provider. Anyone who tried to get Jeremy to follow rules experienced similar problems. So far few people were involved in this aggravating situation, but as years passed, the number of frustrated people grew.

Curious about how things worked ...

At home Jeremy was always taking things apart, curious about how everything worked. Several electronic devices ended up in pieces. I found it almost impossible to stop him from doing something he was determined to do. We had locks on every door, but he was always able to get into things no matter how difficult we made it.

He found ways to access things he wanted to examine. Sometimes he got up in the night, as though he'd deliberately waited until I was asleep.

Since we lived on a farm, I had multiple chores to do every day. We had a large house and barns surrounded by woods. If I diverted my attention for a minute, he would disappear, often creating havoc before I found him. He was cunning and clever, making it difficult to find him when he wanted to get into mischief.

My dad understood my frustration and Jeremy's need to see how things worked. Dad started bringing over old or broken electronic equipment. Speakers, VCRs, computers, typewriters degenerated into piles of chips, wires, screws and small pieces. The cost and effort of hauling remains to the dump was a small price to pay to keep Jeremy occupied.

Editor's Note:

Symptoms of ODD include behaviors that are:

- Persistent
- Disruptive to family and home or school
- Defiant
- Disobedient of rules

Destructive Anger

Nothing was safe ...

By this time Jeremy was not prone to throwing tantrums, yelling, or crying, but bathroom issues and other problems soon developed.

Nothing was safe. Many times it wasn't obvious he was angry or upset. That is, not until I noticed something had been damaged or destroyed. We locked up sharp knives, scissors, and hammers as his destructive behaviors intensified. In spite of locking up sharp implements and tools, he managed to find ways to destroy or damage things.

Over time, I found Jeremy's clothes cut up, beloved trucks and Matchbox cars smashed. He demolished his dresser bit by bit, and broke up his bed. He made slashes in the bedspread, bedding, and mattress. Closet shelves ended up on the floor; molding around the door damaged beyond repair. Walls in his room were riddled with holes.

I made curtains for his window out of fabric he selected. He cut a hole in the cloth and enlarged it until one morning I found the bright-colored material printed with astronomical scenes of planets, moons and stars hanging torn and shredded from the broken rod. Of course he denied doing it.

He found a knife sharp enough to make slashes in a sofa in the basement, and then "painted" it with black shoe polish. We hauled several ruined pieces of furniture to the local landfill during that phase of Jeremy's life.

I couldn't understand why he destroyed things, many of them his favorite possessions. I needed help, but finding help seemed another unachievable goal.

By far the worst ...

By far the worst behavior Jeremy exhibited at this time pertained to toileting issues. He persisted in using his closet as a toilet, totally destroying the carpet. He didn't want to walk down the hall to the bathroom next to his room. His room smelled like a sewer no matter how much cleaning I did to try and keep it clean.

Our master bedroom had a bathroom attached. Jeremy wanted a bathroom in his room like Mommy and Daddy's. He refused to walk to the bathroom next door to his room, insisting on using his closet as a commode. His stubbornness was maddening and baffling.

Our beautiful new custom-built dream home was being deliberately and maliciously damaged beyond repair by one small, determined child. Everything we owned became a target of his unfathomable aggression. Yet I rarely caught him in the throes of his destructive acts.

Time Out was a useless deterrent. Sending him to his room meant more destruction while he was in there. At a friend's recommendation, I tried having him sit in a corner. The wall ended up with holes. I didn't know how he created them.

My dad bought him a punching bag and hung it up in the garage. I tried to encourage Jeremy to go outside and scream at a tree if he was angry. We went out and selected a big fir tree and designated it as his personal screaming tree. He used it a few times, but soon tired of that outlet.

Editor's Note:

Zenia was parenting an angry and resentful four-year-old alone and without an understanding of the source of his anger. Michael continued to work long hours in his medical profession and slept most of the time he was home.

ODD literature states these children perform deliberate actions to annoy others and actively refuse to comply with requests to stop the behavior. Discipline such as Time Out, which Zenia tried, only caused the symptoms to escalate. Her guilt and frustration did not help Jeremy change his behaviors.

Unlocked window ...

Having a bedroom on the main level became a serious problem. I discovered Jeremy could unlock his bedroom window and climb out. The first time that happened, he'd been playing properly in his room while I tended to household tasks. When I went to check on him, he was nowhere to be found. I called his name, called for him, and looked everywhere in the house, finally checking his window. He'd climbed out and pushed it closed from the outside. It hadn't locked.

Jeremy learned he could sneak out and disappear into the woods. With forested land on all four sides it was impossible to know which direction he headed. Had he fallen into a nearby pond? Was he lost in the woods? Fearful scenarios ran through my mind. Eventually, he came to my frantic calls, but he refused to say where he had been.

I planted a spiny pyracantha (firethorn) bush beneath his window hoping it would deter him from sneaking out. A few days later I found most of the branches pruned to the ground.

The end of the school year came; the Montessori program had been a dismal failure. I pre-enrolled Jeremy in kindergarten at a public school with a more structured classroom setting, hoping the next year would be different.

Without the struggle over preschool, summer vacation began somewhat better, though the toilet issue continued. Soon Jeremy found a new target for destruction and a new excuse.

A bird did it...

I went into Jeremy's bedroom to discover broken glass below the window casing.

"A bird did it," Jeremy insisted.

It was a double-pane window and only the inside glass was broken. Jeremy refused to change his story. The cost of damage was adding up. I tried a longer Time Out and kept him in my sight throughout. Now, looking back, I wonder if he spent the time thinking about what to destroy next.

I planned to have old framed window panes I'd collected made into a greenhouse sometime in the future. They were stacked outside against an outbuilding. Jeremy bashed them into thousands of shards of glass. Twenty aquariums stored in a barn met the same fate.

I had been discussing the problems with our pediatrician and related the latest destruction to him. He said Jeremy might have Attention Deficit Hyperactivity Disorder (ADHD) and suggested taking him to a child psychologist.

Michael was adamant our son did not have ADHD, refusing to even consider that possibility. He was totally against taking Jeremy to a psychologist. Since Michael was a doctor, I deferred to his decision.

Parents in conflict ...

Michael was an avid gun collector. His numerous firearms and plentiful supply of ammunition were not kept in a safe. During the first ten years of our marriage, before we had Jeremy, I did not complain too much about them. I didn't use them myself, but I respected his love of target shooting.

Having guns in a home where there are young children was frightening enough. Having a son with Jeremy's behavioral problems where he might access guns was terrifying. Jeremy's pediatrician could not understand my husband, a doctor, being so irresponsible. Guns, at first a point of disagreement in our marriage, were evolving into a serious problem.

Michael started wearing a pistol in a holster at home. One evening at dinner I said, "This is a very bad example to show a young child. Who are you planning on shooting at the dinner table?"

Michael erupted in a screaming rage declaring, "All my friends wear guns to the dinner table."

I never met any of these "friends." He never brought anyone home and didn't talk to anyone on the phone. He did spend time at gun clubs competing in shooting competitions. He had mentioned knowing some of the local police and deputies who frequented the same shooting ranges. I knew they carried sidearms even when off duty. That was a job requirement. I supposed they were the men he was referring to. It didn't matter. They had nothing to do with the issue in our home.

Instead of listening to reason and altering his irresponsible behavior, Michael took another more dangerous tack. He started giving Jeremy shooting lessons.

A friend and I were working in the barn one afternoon while Michael was in charge of Jeremy. We were shocked when we saw my five-year-old son walking through the pasture lugging a rifle and loaded down with bullets carried in bandoliers over his tiny shoulders.

My protests fell on deaf ears. Michael insisted that children needed to be taught how to use a gun to prevent accidents. His argument was that responsible use of weapons was the best way to avoid a problem.

This logic eluded me. Putting a gun in the hands of child with Jeremy's anger issues and destructive behavior was irresponsible in the extreme. Nothing I said made a difference. Jeremy learned how to shoot.

Now I was terrified.

Editor's Note:

Zenia was right to be terrified. While she starts seeking professional guidance for Jeremy, Michael starts exerting his authority as Jeremy's father and a professional with more understanding of professional diagnoses.

The ODD literature suggests that part of the behavior might be the result of incomplete development. Children get stuck in the 2-3 year old stage of child defiance and have trouble outgrowing it.

A learning-based theory suggests the behavior develops as a response to negative interactions. The techniques used by parents and other authority figures to change behaviors with these children do not work as they do with a normal child. Time Out didn't work. Parents in conflict tend to exacerbate behavior problems in their children.

Kindergarten

Brand new teacher ...

I drove Jeremy down the road to meet the school bus for kindergarten. He was very upset about having to go back to school. I was apprehensive, but hoped this year would be different. His kindergarten teacher was brand new, just out of college, starting her first year of teaching. Someone with years of experience would have been preferable. I was afraid she would be unable to handle my son.

It didn't take long before my fears were confirmed. Jeremy resumed his behaviors of the previous year. It became increasingly difficult to get him out of bed. Complaints of sickness were predictable. We were back to the familiar old routine.

I was frequently called in to speak to his teacher. She was unable to get him to follow rules or participate in classroom activities. He sat and watched the other children, and poked and taunted them. His frequent interruptions disrupted the class and irritated his teacher and fellow students. She recommended psychological evaluation and counseling. I returned to Jeremy's pediatrician for a recommendation. He sent us to a reputable child psychologist who mentioned ODD.

21

ODD what? . . .

The child psychologist interviewed Jeremy, Michael and me. He tested our son and explained the results. According to him, Jeremy was borderline ADHD, but the worse problem was Oppositional Defiant Disorder, ODD.

I'd never heard of it. What were we supposed to do? The psychologist wanted to put Jeremy on medication.

Michael was still adamantly opposed to medication. "Jeremy can focus and pay attention; he doesn't have ADHD. I'm not putting him on drugs."

We did not put Jeremy on "drugs", but I agreed, against my husband's wishes, to bring Jeremy back to the clinic for counseling. We had bi-monthly consultations with the psychologist who offered suggestions to alter troubling behaviors. We muddled our way through the opening months of kindergarten with negative reports on his behaviors and social skills.

Before Christmas, Michael told Jeremy, "Santa's elves know you broke your window, and Santa won't bring you as many toys for Christmas if you don't admit you broke it."

Jeremy replied emphatically, "Santa ain't got no elves."

That comment left us laughing hysterically. No confession resulted, but Santa still came and brought toys at Christmas. I wanted my child to be happy. Idle threats exacerbated the problems. I admit I wasn't good at tough love, but I also knew standard discipline didn't work.

Positive Reinforcement . . .

We tried taking toys away and requiring Jeremy to behave as we required to earn them back. He soon preferred to do without. He could earn points for positive behavior that brought rewards, such as going out for pizza. After a couple of times he decided he didn't want to go.

No reward was worth a positive change in his behavior for long. He defied rules at all cost, preferring to do without things he would have loved and subjecting himself to discipline the psychologist suggested rather than give in to authority. Any improvements were minor and short-lived. No discipline was severe enough and no reward great enough to make any difference. It defied logic.

I'd learned that sending him to his room for time-out didn't work. I tried putting him in a bare corner to think, as suggested by the psychologist. That met with increasing retaliation. All the laminate countertops in my new kitchen were damaged. Jeremy cut little grooves all the way around the edges with a sharp knife. He perforated walls with an ice pick he'd found, and used a rock to etch scrawls on a picture window in the dining room. He painted window screens, or cut them and smashed downspouts.

We tried to keep sharp tools locked up in tool boxes, in a safe, or behind locked doors. Every door in our house had a lock, but Jeremy managed to jimmy the locks or to find the keys and hide them. I still have chests and curio cabinets without keys lost during that time.

My husband Michael had finally made one major concession and purchased a very large, heavy duty gun safe, agreeing that Jeremy might be able to access other locked storage. At last the guns and a bayonet collection were safely locked away. Michael had previously stopped wearing the holstered gun around the house.

That concern was alleviated. I think the ODD diagnosis got Michael's attention.

Jeremy's destructive acts almost always occurred while I was tending to our farm animals or when he went on nighttime forays while I slept. I tried tying a string around my wrist and his so he would stay by my side, but that made most tasks impossible. He disappeared as soon as I released him to complete farm tasks. He refused to stay with me. His defiance of rules continually escalated.

Editor's Note:

The ODD literature concludes that the main treatment for children with this disorder is parental management. Parents need to improve their parenting skills in ways specific to the individual child's needs. The program needs to be designed specific to the child.

Many ODD children also have Attention Deficit Hyperactivity Disorder (ADHD) and are helped by medication. In recent years, some nutritional supplements have proved helpful.

Zenia continued to bow to Michael's refusal to let Jeremy be treated with drugs.

First Grade

A male teacher ...

First grade began on a positive note. I was pleased to meet Jeremy's new teacher, a man this time, and marveled at how well he controlled his young charges. They clustered around him like chicks following a mother hen, hanging on his every word. I was optimistic.

It wasn't long before my bubble of optimism burst. Jeremy's teacher called me in for a discussion. He was stymied by my son's lack of cooperation, refusal to follow instructions, disruptive interruptions, and continued irritation of classmates. All the same behaviors had carried over from the previous year. It was disheartening. My hopes for a good year dissipated.

The point system ...

Our psychologist suggested using the point system at school. His teacher agreed, willing to try any method, and started keeping track of points. Unfortunately, this had the same very short period of positive results it had at home. Jeremy responded positively to change, but once things got old, his familiar habits returned and he reverted to his uncooperative self. He spent his school time watching classmates work, while he refused to participate. His teacher joined the growing list of frustrated educators.

Jeremy was put into an Individualized Education Program (IEP) and given limited Special Ed status. This allowed him to conform to lower expectations then the majority of students, and he was given closer supervision and assistance, mostly concerned with organization. He was actually quite bright, and was not mentally incapable of learning. He had ongoing behavioral problems that needed to be addressed.

Jeremy liked to eat lunch with his school guidance counselor. She spent quite a bit of time with him, and he had a very positive relationship with her. She saw him often, and made suggestions to his teachers and me.

Getting to eat lunch with her was offered as a reward. While helpful, this had little impact on the final outcome. As usual, rewards had a very short-term positive effect. Nothing worked for more than a few times. Once Jeremy got used to something, the newness wore off and it no longer mattered—good or bad.

At home, we got a new puppy, Chester, a Pomeranian to replace one stomped beneath a horse's hooves. Jeremy spent a lot of time with the new pup, carting him around in his wagon. His behavior with the dog seemed appropriate, but somehow Chester's leg was broken and needed a cast.

On a follow-up checkup to the vet, pebbles were discovered inside the cast.

"How did rocks get inside the cast?" the vet asked.

I said, "I don't know." That wasn't true. I was certain Jeremy had put them there.

An accomplished liar ...

I returned home with the dog, a new cast on his leg, and lectured Jeremy on being kind to animals, but I doubted it would have any effect. Jeremy adamantly denied doing it.

By now my child was an accomplished liar who rarely told the truth. He was so adept, he'd look me right in the eye and lie. It was impossible to know he wasn't telling the truth. He lied about inconsequential things, when there was absolutely no reason, just to do it. I couldn't believe anything he said. Everything was a fabrication. He made up complex stories about school incidents that never occurred.

Destruction continues ...

Jeremy had a large sand pile where he spent countless hours constructing drainage and irrigation systems out of pieces of pipe. Christmas was just around the corner and he had prepared a list for Santa, a stack of pictures cut from catalogs and newspaper ads. He wanted dump trucks and road graders to work in his sand.

Christmas day he was thrilled when he opened his packages and both families of grandparents had given him big dump trucks and road graders. The heavy metal Tonka set was especially impressive. He spent a few days delighted with his new toys before I discovered the smashed remnants in the yard. He admitted bashing them with a sledgehammer. No matter how much he treasured his possessions, they always ended up in the same condition—ruined. I couldn't tell our parents.

One weekend I took Jeremy to a rabbit show held at a National Guard armory in another state. He went outside to play with the other kids.

Someone came inside to get me and tell me, "Jeremy took apart a concrete wall, and he broke up the blocks."

I surveyed the damage, shocked by the senseless destruction, and confronted my son.

"I didn't do it!"

Several people pointed at him and said they saw him do it.

"It wasn't me. It was someone who looked just like me."

A young mother laughed. "Right, it wasn't you. It was your evil twin."

"Yeah," he answered, readily accepting that for an excuse.

I cleaned the mess, and helped rebuild the wall as well as we could with the broken pieces. They requested that I refrain from bringing Jeremy to any more shows. I was devastated and embarrassed. How could my child behave so badly? He was so unlike any child I had ever been around. Positive reinforcement and other behavior changing methods suggested by the psychologist were failing. I felt powerless and hopeless.

Need for control...

At home, I was still trying to solve toilet issues. His room was ghastly. I had him doing push-ups or jumping jacks, a suggested consequence. One time I said, "Do fifty jumping jacks."

"No, I won't. I'll do a hundred, and I'll do them standing on the sofa."

This was harsher than the consequence I applied, but that didn't matter. Everything had to be his idea.

"I'll do a hundred push-ups and a hundred jumping jacks," he added another time.

He had to be in control. ODD is a strange behavior. It defies logic. He often increased imposed penalties as long as the idea was his.

I tried having him clean up his own toileting messes, but that failed to achieve the desired results. He still refused to use the bathroom, and his unsatisfactory cleaning job left his room worse than before he started. I still had to clean up after him.

My husband and I had lived overseas for years and I had many expensive items that had survived intact through several moves. They couldn't outlast my son. One treasure after another ended up damaged. I developed the philosophy they were just things, and I had to mentally detach myself from them.

I remembered a physician teacher from Michael's medical school telling me years before that children were 'guests in their parents' home. They had to behave and follow rules." That model didn't fit our family at all. Jeremy had no respect for other people's possessions, and he ignored boundaries and limits we tried to impose.

He still drew on walls and floors with permanent markers, damaged wood trim around doors, and kept up his assault on our house and possessions.

Finally, he admitted to one of his destructive behaviors—the smashed taillights on a car.

"Dad said that car was a piece of junk."

I told him never to do that again.

A new scratch gleamed along the side of my car one day and the back window was shattered as it sat parked in the garage. Jeremy denied involvement.

I again tried keeping him with me at all times with a long line attached to each of our wrists. This effort was as unsuccessful as prior attempts. As soon as I separated us, he took off.

We started replacing furniture items we liked with items we found in thrift stores. We patched and repainted his room. I bought a used bright red dresser. Jeremy hated it, but I refused to buy him a nice one again. It was well-made of wood and a child somewhere had probably treasured it, but it was doomed to an inglorious demise in our home.

He caused so much damage and destruction at such a young age, I dreaded the future, worrying about what he would be capable of doing as he got older. How could a child so young be capable of such malicious behavior?

Blame the Mother ...

One of my lowest points came on a morning Jeremy helped me gather trash and load it into the pickup for a trip to the dump. It was a school day. I said, "You're going to have to stop helping now. It's time to get ready for school."

He went inside the house without saying anything. I followed. He disappeared into the walk-in pantry. I went in to get him and he had urinated all over the food on my shelves.

I was beyond upset. After dropping him off at the school bus, I phoned my parents and told them what he'd done—something I seldom did. They didn't know how much difficulty I was having with their grandson or the range of his misbehaviors.

A few days later I received a letter from each of my parents telling me how my son was "crying out for attention." My mother had found a pediatric psychiatrist in their area. She said she'd "explained the whole situation to the doctor" and would pay for Jeremy's visits to him.

I called her and my father to explain that we were seeing a psychologist, what he'd diagnosed and how we were approaching the problem. No way was I going to an additional doctor whose knowledge of the case had been tainted by my mother's opinions.

Michael wasn't much more help than my mother. He refused to attend sessions with the psychologist and Jeremy's discipline was left entirely to me. It would have helped to have someone back me up at home. Without assistance, I was fighting a losing battle.

My mother-in-law, aware of the problems, blamed me and said to me, "You are the only one Jeremy has any problem with. *You* are the problem."

Other adults...

That wasn't true of course. Jeremy had problems with his teachers, school bus drivers, and any adults in the role of setting limits and making him follow rules. Jeremy was very nice to people who didn't expect anything of him.

For Jeremy, sitting still on a school bus and getting along with other riders was a constant battle. He was ordered to sit up front where the driver could keep an eye on him. Worse than that, he was often suspended from riding the bus for days at a time. He considered this a reward—he hated riding the bus, and much preferred having me drive him the nine-mile round trip twice a day.

We enrolled him in Cub Scouts. I thought doing crafts and activities with other boys would be good for his social development. I'd been a Brownie and a Girl Scout and enjoyed the experience.

Cub Scouts, unlike Brownies, didn't do crafts. The boys were rowdy, loud, and unruly. Jeremy didn't like the activities pursued, so the involvement in the organization proved to be a negative experience. One year was enough. Jeremy didn't want to go anymore and we agreed.

Editor's Note:

The DSM IV list of diagnostic criteria include behaviors Zenia sees increasingly in Jeremy. At this point in his development, he is often exhibiting the following:

- Argues with adults
- Actively defies or refuses to comply with adults' requests or rules
- Deliberately annoys people
- Blames others for his misbehavior
- Is angry and resentful
- Is spiteful or vindictive

The information states the behaviors do not occur only during the course of what might be diagnosed as a psychotic or mood disorder episode.

Second Grade

Concentrate on behavior ...

Jeremy's second grade teacher was a very charismatic, talented young man. I was nervous when I saw how young he looked, but he assured me he had been teaching for six years. After a short period of time, he let me know he was going to concentrate on behavioral issues not academics.

Jeremy really liked him and enjoyed being in his class. That was a first, but that didn't mean he wanted to go to school. Nor did he become cooperative.

The class was structured around the reward system with each student working on a journal to earn a field trip. I urged Jeremy to finish his, and he came very close. His teacher gave him until the morning of the trip, and even called me at home that morning in the hope it was complete. I told him it was not. His teacher was disappointed. He said all Jeremy's classmates had been pulling for him, hoping he would get to go. He had nearly finished, but refused to make a final effort to get it done. The teacher didn't make an exception to the rule for Jeremy. While all his classmates went on the outing, Jeremy remained at school with another class.

His own worst enemy ...

My heart ached for my son. It hurt that he was his own worst enemy. He couldn't see that his annoying habits hurt no one more than himself. I wanted the best for him and continued to try practicing the suggestions from his psychologist to encourage Jeremy to change his behavior. Taking away his favorite toys and having him earn them back or offering special outings did not work for long.

The week before a meeting with his teacher, Jeremy told me his teacher had been standing on a table, fell off and broke his leg. He told me they had a substitute. I went to my appointment the next week and was surprised to see the teacher in perfect condition. I was stunned.

"Your leg isn't broken."

"No. Should it be?" He looked puzzled.

I repeated the story Jeremy told me. He shook his head, amazed that my son had come up with that scenario in the hope it would prevent me from meeting with him.

Then he asked why I never responded to notes he sent home with Jeremy.

"What notes? I never got any notes."

He nodded, understanding what had happened. "I'll call you if I need to communicate with you," he said.

Later when I confronted Jeremy about notes from his teacher, a friend of his overheard us talking. He said, "Jeremy ate notes on the bus so he wouldn't have to give them to you."

I was flabbergasted. "Is that true? You ate notes from your teacher rather than give them to me?"

"Yeah."

"Don't do it again. If your teacher sends a note home, I want to see it. I want you to bring it to me."

"OOOkaaayyy!"

I really didn't count on him to bring me notes. The school made sure all future communication with me was done by phone. If they had to send something in writing, they called to tell me ahead of time so I knew when to ask Jeremy for it.

Over the years I continued to receive frequent calls from his counselors, teachers, and even the principal.

Ritalin prescribed ...

Teachers and psychologists wanted us to have Jeremy put on medication to help control his behavior and enhance his ability to learn. His pediatrician prescribed Ritalin. The pills made him sick and didn't improve his behavior. My husband was still opposed to the use of Ritalin or any other drug of that type. We told the school he would not continue medication.

The advice of friends ...

Still battling the toilet problem, I decided to try a new plan. Since Jeremy insisted he needed a bathroom in his bedroom, I moved him into the bathroom on a bed made up on the floor. This did solve the main issue; he used the toilet. But the bathroom trim and doors were scarred, and the floor was marked up. It seemed to me he was exerting his control. He'd use the toilet, but he'd do a different kind of damage. I had to return him to his room where he reverted to using his closet.

Though toileting issues in children Jeremy's age are linked to the need to control others and to emotional problems, I still don't understand why he fought my parental authority in such an extreme way. I continued following professional advice until Jeremy went with me to visit a friend. With her permission, he used the bathroom there.

She called me, angry and upset, shortly after we returned home. My son had urinated on the walls and floor in my friend's bathroom. She told me he was not welcome and never to bring him there again. I was horrified. As deplorable as his behavior was at home, he had never done anything like that in another person's house.

As his behavior worsened, I became more desperate. Finally, I divulged that dirty little secret to more friends, hoping someone would have a solution that our years in counseling had been unable to provide.

One friend, a grandmother, said I should try rubbing his nose in the urine like housebreaking a puppy. That sounded extreme so I didn't consider it.

Several other friends suggested swatting Jeremy's backside with a switch. I hadn't wanted to do that because my own mother had regularly used a stick on me. I was determined not to be an abusive parent.

One friend understood my feeling about spanking but insisted it might be worth trying.

"Have him go outside and pick out the switch himself. Part of the punishment is having him think about it. Besides he will pick out a very small switch."

The next time I found urine in his room I tried the suggestion. He was clearly unhappy about the punishment and chose a tiny willow twig. It didn't have much impact on cloth-padded butt, and it did nothing to alter his behavior.

Another spiteful behavior ...

About that time Jeremy developed another spiteful behavior. My dad came to help me with house and farm needs. Jeremy always liked helping Grandpa. When Dad went to leave, he noticed an upturned nail behind his driver's side front tire. He checked the other tires and found a nail behind each one. He was furious and told Jeremy he would never come back if it happened again.

My dad's car was safe, but a friend who'd stopped by had two flat tires soon afterward. He recognized the nails as coming from our place. Of course Jeremy denied having anything to do with it. His behaviors increasingly isolated us from friends and family.

Editor's Note:

ODD children often deliberately annoy people, even people who don't try to impose rules or expectations on them. There is no known clear cause of Oppositional Defiant Disorder. It may be a combination of inherited and environmental factors and may include:
- limitations or developmental delays in a child's ability to process thoughts and feelings
- an imbalance of certain brain chemicals, such as serotonin

Third Grade

Sitting on a box...

Second grade ended with Jeremy passed on to third in spite of failing grades and dismal behavioral evaluations. He was assigned to another male teacher, who made little headway with him.

Jeremy spent a lot of class time sitting on a box watching fellow students work. The teacher also sent him out into the hall, away from other students. Jeremy considered that a reward. I asked his teacher to make him do push-ups, or anything that was an applied consequence that also released some energy.

"I can't do that," the teacher said. "It's cruel and unusual punishment and is against school policy."

Other problems continued developing at school. I got a phone call from the principal, who sounded exasperated. "Jeremy was caught running on the playground again."

"What's wrong with that?"

"Children aren't permitted to run on the playground area. He might bump into someone and get hurt, or hurt someone else. We are suspending him from recess."

While that was sinking in, I thought about school when I was growing up. We'd go to school early to play before class, and stay late to play after school. Now, playground was off limits except for recess, and running was supposedly banned. I was disgusted with the rule and upset about Jeremy's suspension. Running was one of the few things that helped settle him down, and now it was forbidden.

In my day, kids got into fights on the playground. Some kids fought on a regular basis. As far as I know, no one was ever punished for fighting.

Times had changed.

A couple of weeks later Jeremy came home bragging "I told my friends to poop and pee on the floor to get even with their parents."

"Why did you do that?" I was appalled. It was inconceivable.

"Because—"

"What did their parents do?"

He snickered. "They got in trouble. Won't do it again."

I was never able to find out who those children were or what their parents did to punish them.

That my son had been proud of this behavior and had actually encouraged other kids to follow his advice was astounding—and had to be stopped—no matter what.

I remembered my friend's suggestion about house-breaking him like a puppy? Rub his nose in it. Maybe it was worth a try. Nothing else was working.

Breakthrough with Consequences...

He urinated on the floor in his room again. This time I followed my friend's advice and rubbed his nose in it. Feelings of guilt were short-lived. He never went to the bathroom in his room again. I was elated. The disciplinary action proved to be successful. On our next visit to the psychologist, I explained what I had done and how it had corrected our long-standing toilet issue.

"I have to report that to Child Protective Services," he informed me.

"Oh that's just great." I suffer the consequence for using a disciplinary action that finally corrected a horrible problem that lasted for years.

A young man came from CPS came to interview Jeremy and me. I explained the history of our problem, and, in anger and frustration, said, "If you think I'm doing a bad job with him, you can take him." Children are removed from abusive parents, and the report filed by the psychologist indicated abuse.

"Oh no! No! You're not an abusive parent, just a very frustrated one. I don't know what I'd do if I had a child like that. I don't know what to tell you, but I'll send you some information on Oppositional Defiant Disorder."

I received the information in the mail; beyond confirming that Jeremy fit the behaviors on the diagnostic scale, it wasn't particularly helpful.

The CPS representative had been insistent that I wasn't an abusive parent or a bad mother, just a frustrated one. I put it all behind me. (At least I thought I had until it came back to haunt me in an unexpected way eleven years later.)

Deteriorating marriage...

By this time my marriage was deteriorating. Michael moved out three weeks before Christmas of Jeremy's third grade year. My son and I were on our own.

We had a peaceful Christmas—our first. It helped me realize what a verbally abusive person my husband had become. Most everything he did involved a lot of yelling, even screaming. I attributed it to the demands of his work and long hours, and coming home to endure Jeremy's ongoing behaviors.

Jeremy and I cut down a tree, put it up in the stand and decorated it without a cross word. We had a great time decorating our tree. We made special ornaments, an activity Jeremy enjoyed. He hung garlands everywhere.

Jeremy said, "This was the best time we ever had putting up our Christmas tree."

We made lots of Christmas cookies together. Jeremy loved squeezing out spritz cookies, putting on colored sprinkles, cutting out sugar cookies with cookie cutters and painting sugar cookies with colored frosting. My family came over for Christmas dinner. It was a memorable year. We got through the holiday season without any major mishaps.

Creative Energy . . .

Jeremy's desire to make things seemed like positive progress to me. He took an interest in sewing. We sewed a pair of shorts for him. I bought buttons shaped like animals. He painted white fabric with background scenes and sewed on the animal buttons. He helped me sew a special red apron with Noah's Ark animals on it. He loved wearing the clothes he'd helped sew.

He joined a friend and me on a trip to a ceramic shop where he selected bisque, fired, unglazed clay projects to glaze. Dinosaurs were a favorite. He liked wearing his special red apron, painting glazes on the bisque and having it fired.

His interest led to the purchase of our own kiln, pouring table, and molds. We did ceramics at home in the basement. Jeremy poured slip into molds and made little animals. He helped load and unload the kiln and spent hours glazing his work.

In spite of the many good times we had during that year, his defiant behavior continued at school and his academic success did not improve.

New counselor ...

Jeremy's psychologist told us he couldn't be of any more help. He'd done what he could. He recommended we see another counselor at his clinic, one he thought more suited to Jeremy's needs.

I liked Ben immediately. He was a hardcore former Marine, tough, with a different approach and he was used to counseling the most difficult children. I told him about being turned in to CPS by his associate.

"You should never have been turned in for child abuse. I don't report parents. The kids I see are the abusers."

The abuser comment both surprised and troubled me, and triggered a memory. There were a few times in first and second grade when Jeremy had threatened to beat me with a broom handle or large walking stick. They were idle threats that I'd ignored. Ignoring some behaviors was considered a behavior modification technique.

Jeremy took an instant dislike to his new counselor. He stood glaring in front of Ben, arms straight, fists clenched, contorting his face into the meanest expressions he could muster.

Ben grinned at him. "You're a real Jekyll and Hyde. I just watched you turn from an angelic-looking kid into an evil-looking monster. You don't fool me. I see your type all the time."

On one visit Ben told him, "You don't know how lucky you are to have your mom. I see a lot of kids whose parents beat the crap out of them. There are parents out there who would have killed you by now."

Hearing Ben say that shocked me. Still, I could imagine parents driven to murder. Would they plead temporary insanity? Kids could be horrible. Mine was certainly trying to push me over the edge. With his dad gone, I was on my own. Even though Michael had not been much help, raising Jeremy alone was a daunting task.

Rearing him was a challenge that often left me feeling sad, depressed and frustrated. I wondered how other parents would deal with something like this. How would they cope? Would one of them walk out on the family as Michael had done?

Intelligence factors...

A bulldozer operator working on a property down the road came to do some work for me while he was in the area. Jeremy had been wandering away to watch him work. The operator was kind enough to stop his rig for chats.

"How old is your son?" he asked.

"Eight," I replied, expecting him to say I needed to keep Jeremy from interrupting his work.

He laughed. "Eight going on eighteen. He was telling me all about how diesel machinery operates, and how my dozer works."

I wasn't surprised. Jeremy loved machines and all sorts of devices. He'd spent hours taking apart things my dad and others found for him. He loved to read about how those things worked.

Fourth Grade

Custody change ...

Like all divorcing couples, Michael and I haggled over our divorce settlement, division of property and child custody. He had a new girlfriend and was planning on getting married soon. He realized he had made many parenting mistakes. In fact, he had done very little parenting. He believed that he and his new wife could do a better job of raising Jeremy than I could alone.

I agonized over my dilemma. I didn't want to give up my son, but with his failing grades at school, maybe living with his father was the best choice. Michael found a private school for Jeremy and took him to a psychologist for more tests. Jeremy scored very high on an intelligence test. Neither one of us was surprised.

I gave in, placing hope on the private school and belief that Jeremy needed his dad's involvement. We agreed to have Michael take physical custody of Jeremy. I would have him twice a month on weekends.

Our divorce hadn't been finalized when I packed up most of Jeremy's things and sent him off to live with his dad. Two weeks later I met Michael to pick up Jeremy for the weekend. Michael told me Jeremy wasn't getting along with his new stepmother, Brenda.

Soon after that, she called me to discuss problems she was having with my son. During that conversation she said, "Jeremy told me, 'I tortured my mom.' He brags about it."

I wasn't sure what she wanted me to say about that or what Jeremy meant. He didn't physically torture me, but maybe he had an understanding of psychological torture. His intelligence factor made that possible. I wasn't sure if that was the case, or if he was trying to frighten his stepmother in some way. In any case, she refused to be left alone with him.

Male nanny ...

Michael hired a male nanny to take care of our son. Much of the time, Jeremy stayed at the nanny's house. Brenda refused to be alone with Jeremy. Michael refused to give me the nanny's telephone number and forbid me from calling his home to talk with Jeremy.

He had been much nicer and easier to deal with as well as open in our discussions about Jeremy after he moved out of our home, but with his new wife in the picture everything changed. I had no contact either physical or by phone with Jeremy other than our bimonthly visits.

I contacted my attorney, concerned about Jeremy spending time with a nanny I'd never met, and about my inability to talk with Jeremy between our visits.

The attorney understood my concern. He advised me that even though Michael had primary custody, Jeremy didn't have to actually live with him. "You agreed to your ex-husband taking custody. You cannot get Jeremy back on those grounds."

Every two weeks I'd see Jeremy for the weekend. He arrived unhappy, cried a lot and said he wanted to come back to live with me. He hated Brenda and missed me, and promised he'd be good if he could come home. He said he'd be "real bad" around his dad and stepmother so they'd let him come back to live with me. I explained as best I could that he had to stay with his dad and told him he needed to behave.

At the end of the weekend visits, he cried the entire hour and a half drive to meet his dad or the nanny.

Custody change two...

In the spring, as the school year was drawing to an end, I received a fax from Michael. It informed me that he, as primary custodial parent, was sending Jeremy to a boarding school in New Hampshire. He said I had to contribute $1000 a month to help pay for Jeremy's expenses.

I called my former mother-in-law (who had previously said all my problems with Jeremy were my fault) hoping she'd help me get Jeremy back. I didn't want him sent to New Hampshire where, financially, I'd be unable to visit him.

She said, "Jeremy is a sociopath. There is no hope for him. He needs to be sent away."

I contacted my attorney who said Michael couldn't send our son out of the state without my permission. He added, "Now is the time to petition to regain custody of Jeremy."

When I went to my attorney's office to finalize custody paperwork, I learned it specified Michael would not see Jeremy on weekends or holidays unless he requested it ahead of time.

I said, "He should see Jeremy at least once a month."

"You can't make him see his son," the attorney said.

The lawyer's secretary had tears in her eyes as I was leaving. "That is the saddest custody agreement I have ever seen." She said, "Never show it to your son."

When we met for me to pick up Jeremy, Michael said, "He can never come back to my house."

"What are you talking about? You can request visits." I couldn't believe what he was saying.

"He and Brenda don't get along. I can't have him in my house."

How could he mean that? How could any woman refuse to allow her husband to see his child?

I put a bag of clothes into my trunk. "Where are the rest of his things?"

"I got rid of them."

"What?"

"I gave them all away."

"What about his PlayStation and music keyboard? They were gifts from my parents."

"He didn't deserve them. I had a friend who wanted them." He looked away.

I said, "You can take things away, to change behavior, but he should be allowed to earn them back." When he didn't reply, I asked, "What did he have to do at your house?"

"Read . . . he had books."

"Is that all? He couldn't do anything but read?"

"That's right."

I regretted sending all of Jeremy's things with him when he went to live with his dad. I was never able to find out what really went on there. That ten month period remains a mystery to me. But it changed Jeremy forever.

The only good report cards Jeremy ever got were from the private school he attended in the fourth grade while living with Michael. Other consequences were not so wonderful. The worst aftermath was intense dislike of reading. His one-time love affair with books was over. He refused to read anything. Getting him to study, never easy, became virtually impossible. He refused to read almost everything except repair manuals and instruction guides. Reading for pleasure was a thing of the past.

Editor's Note:

The causes or reasons for ODD are still not clearly understood, but studies suggest there is a familial link. The role of genetics is unclear. These children often lack cognitive or emotional skills for their age level. They particularly lack organized problem solving skills.

Children with both ODD and ADHD tend to be more aggressive, have more persistent behavioral problems and are more likely to underachieve academically.

New role models ...

When Jeremy came back home in June, I sought more positive male role models to fill the niche never really provided by his father. I believed encouraging him to form friendships with other boys would be beneficial and thought it would give him a better chance to fit in when he started fifth grade in his public school in September.

We attended the Assembly of God Church where a number of men took an interest in Jeremy's socialization, working with him in Royal Rangers. He competed in the pinewood derby with a car he built and painted by himself. Of course he had refused all help. His car didn't look as nice as the others, but he was proud of it.

He went off to Royal Ranger summer camp, where he had his typical difficulties getting along. Reluctantly, the director allowed him to stay, but getting him to attend church after that became a struggle. He didn't want to be around the other boys who'd attended camp.

Jeremy always seemed to get along better with adults, particularly men, than he did with boys his own age. I grew tired of arguing with him every Sunday. He always claimed to be sick. I finally gave up. Jeremy wore me down again.

Next we joined the local Mycological Society. Jeremy was the only child at meetings attended largely by elderly people at that time. He was very popular with them. He was helpful and even prepared snacks or food for club potlucks. When we decided to have monthly lectures on a "mushroom of the month," Jeremy volunteered to present the first one. He selected a species, *Boletus zelleri*, did the research and gave a wonderful oral presentation on Zeller's Bolete, an edible mushroom that grows in the woods near our house.

Jeremy loved hiking and camping in the woods, searching for mushrooms. He was one of only two boys on forays. He became an expert at locating mushrooms, and still does a much better job of finding them than I do.

My dad, who came weekly to help me with household tasks, started commenting about the things that needed to be repaired or replaced. He shook his head. "All your child support is going to have to be used to pay for damages."

He was right. I needed to find more activities to occupy Jeremy in positive ways.

Working with his hands...

Jeremy had a natural artistic talent, one not shared by me, which I encouraged. I bought him pastel artist chalk, water colors and other supplies. It was a positive way of getting him to express his emotions. Art was something he enjoyed in every form. He drew wonderful pictures of our farm.

He also enjoyed visiting a neighbor's construction site where he was allowed to collect discarded materials. He carted home several wagon-loads of pipes and spent countless hours creating a drainage system in his sand pile. He told everyone he was going to be a plumber when he grew up.

I hired a company to log five acres on a parcel of land next to our house. The loggers let him join them in their work, taking him aboard their heavy equipment. He participated in cutting down a tree with the cutter. Large claws grasped the tree while a saw blade sliced through the trunk. When the logging ended, the equipment operator let Jeremy help drive the equipment down our dirt road.

My son had a new love. "I'm gonna be a logger," he bragged.

Jeremy's interests all involved working with his hands. He gravitated toward men who were blue-collar workers, men who epitomized his new ideal. I recognized the irony. Their work and his father's were opposite ends of a scale.

He found "working men," as they called themselves, willing to take him under their wings. Jeremy preferred them to the playmates his age. Surprisingly, these older companions enjoyed his company. They explained what they were doing, imparting a wealth of information he absorbed and remembered.

He was given odd jobs at the construction site near us. He performed cleanup and gopher tasks, and he took pride in his duties. I no longer had to wonder where he'd gone when he slipped away. He had permission to visit the site as long as the work crew knew he was there, and he followed their rules.

I had frequent conversations with his numerous mentors. We agreed that they were to send him home if he got in their way or annoyed them. Every one said he was no problem. They enjoyed his company. He was never sent home. I was amazed.

Permission: the "P" Word...

After the divorce, due to reduced finances mentioned, I cancelled our second phone line. Jeremy heard me say I didn't need a line just for the computer. Shortly after the change, the phone had an echo.

"Something's wrong with the phone," I said, as I looked for the number to call the phone company."

Jeremy had a strange look on his face. "I think I know what the problem is." He headed for the door.

"What do you mean you know what the problem is? What did you do?"

"I disconnected the second phone line."

"I did not tell you to do that. Don't do anything without permission. Remember the 'P' word."

"OOOkkkaaaayyyy!"

The "P" word was a constant source of aggravation between us. Though he followed workmen's rules, he ignored mine. He was always damaging things in our home in the process of "fixing" them. Most things weren't in need of repair until he got to them. As far as he was concerned, nothing was off limits if it was on our property.

I still don't understand that. Jeremy wanted to be home with me. He enjoyed creative activities I provided, but he seemed unable to resist taking things apart to see how they worked.

Fifth & sixth grades

Inflexible teacher ...

Jeremy returned to his original school and entered the fifth grade in a split-grade class taught by a woman. The two of them clashed from the start, which didn't bode well for the academic year. I made frequent visits to his class for discussions with her regarding dealing with Jeremy. We disagreed on a number of issues. She was totally inflexible and found dealing with a child who didn't fit the mold a formidable challenge. She expected all homework assignments to be turned in on time. No exceptions. Failure to do so resulted in suspension of recess privileges. Jeremy seldom got to go out for recess.

When she discovered a hand-drawn portrait of herself wearing a witch's pointed hat and long black dress on the back of a homework assignment, things went from bad to worse. All my attempts to have him removed from her class, a resolution I believed would benefit both of them, were unsuccessful. I was certain another teacher would better able to cope with the challenge of dealing with him and she certainly disliked having him in her class.

One morning Jeremy cut his hair, not the first time he'd done it, but this cut was the worst. He'd cut it very short with grooves running from front to back clear down to the scalp. The principal called and refused to allow him in class looking like that. I had to go pick him up, find a hair salon that could fit him in immediately, and have his haircut repaired. The stylists joked about how that was the worst haircut they'd ever seen. The beautician did her best, but it was impossible to do a great job with what was left. It was good enough to get him back in school.

Money making plan...

In December, unbeknownst to me, Jeremy came up with a plan to make money selling Christmas trees. I discovered a large pile of Douglas fir trees cut and heaped on the basement floor. He'd cut down over thirty trees that were seven feet tall. He knew I wanted them to grow. Of course he hadn't asked permission; the "P" word again. Now they were wasted. I ordered him to haul the trees out back and stack them in a pile out behind the pasture.

Jeremy couldn't wait for Christmas. He decorated the house for the holidays. Garlands were stapled to the walls and hung everywhere, of course without permission. He drew a picture of Santa Claus and left it beside a glass of milk and plate of cookies for Santa. He was thrilled that Santa took the picture with him. (I still have it saved somewhere.)

Michael agreed to see Jeremy for a couple of days over the holiday season. He drove from his home three hours away. They stayed in a motel. That was their only time together until summer, when they went for what was to become a ritual week of camping every August.

School bus suspensions...

I went back to school in a re-careering move and tried to be a positive role model. I hoped Jeremy would follow my example and keep up with his homework. Of course, that didn't happen. Somehow he survived the school year, but his grades returned to their dismal level.

He disliked the school bus driver and was frequently suspended from riding the bus. He much preferred having me drive him to school rather than riding the hated bus. He was jubilant whenever his misbehavior resulted in suspension from the bus.

I confided this problem to a friend who'd had a similar experience. She had two sons, and made one walk part way to school when he was suspended off the bus. She said that stopped the problem.

It sounded like a good idea, so I took her advice. We started out doing one half mile and upped it to one mile as he got older and reasons for suspension got worse. I'd drive along the side of the road beside him, and let him in after he'd walked far enough. Sometimes other drivers, people I didn't even know, would slow down to yell at me for being so cruel to my child, making him walk.

I often wondered how other parents would react if they had to put up with behaviors I'd been living with almost since my son's birth.

Jeremy managed to acquire a few friends, usually girls. He had trouble getting along with boys his age. He still loved hanging out with men, particularly construction workers, loggers, heavy equipment operators, plumbers and electricians. He managed to find new houses being built nearby and would be allowed to sweep floors, pick up nails, pieces of pipe, boards, or roofing. He was always bringing home remnants from these sites. He'd spend hours constructing complex systems in his sand pile.

One time he got suspended from the school bus for having nails in his pocket.

"What's wrong with that?" I asked the principal.

"Nails are weapons, just like rubber bands," the principal answered.

"But he wasn't using them as a weapon. They were in his pocket."

"He showed them to someone."

"Oh well, that explains it." I hung up the phone in frustration.

The next time I spoke to the principal, he phoned to tell me Jeremy was being suspended from school for bringing hardcore pornography to school and showing it to kids on the bus and on the school grounds. I was stunned. He and a friend had downloaded it off the internet.

I banned his friend from our house. I tried putting Jeremy on restriction, but as usual he climbed out the window and disappeared. Taking away privileges or personal possessions and having him earn them back was the only thing that provided even modest success in dealing with Jeremy's behavioral issues. At least there were no more incidents with pornography.

His sixth grade teacher, a woman he actually liked, managed to get him to do fairly well in school. She recognized that he was very bright and encouraged him to work on assignments that were of interest to him. He didn't earn any A's, but at least his grades were satisfactory. Best of all, there were no F's.

One afternoon, I went into the kitchen to discover Jeremy had made a blue volcano, something he'd learned in school. He never told me how he made it, but it was one big mess. He created it on the kitchen counter, where it erupted, spewing bright, blue, wet "lava" all over the countertop, cupboards, and floor. Needless to say, it took me several hours to clean up the mess.

I noticed an odd smell emanating from his room and discovered a very active mold colony flourishing on a damp "town" made out of flour and water paste. It was constructed on my best new baking pan. Another lecture on the use of the "P" word resulted, but I knew it was futile. Permission was never required as far as Jeremy was concerned.

The last two weeks of school, Jeremy was suspended from the bus for telling the bus driver he would shoot her with a 12-guage shot gun. He didn't have one, and with Michael gone there were no guns in our house.

I had to leave early every other morning to drive to my own school, so the principal was kind enough to pick up Jeremy and drive him to school on the days I was gone. He actually liked Jeremy and sympathized with my situation.

The school had a half-day near the end, and the principal decided rather than drive Jeremy that morning, he would let him stay home.

Jeremy was riding his bike, caught the wheel on the edge of the blacktop and flipped into the side of a car. He smashed the mirror with his face, knocking out a front tooth. Fortunately, a nurse lived nearby and came to the scene. She found the tooth, and plunked it into a glass of milk. It survived implantation. He was black-and-blue all over and spent a couple of days lying around the house, but luckily, he had no other injuries.

If he hadn't been suspended from the bus and getting rides with the principal, he wouldn't have been riding his bike alone. That repaired tooth was shorter and out of alignment with the rest of his teeth, but at least it was still there and alive.

We were supposed to go camping with the mycological society the next weekend, but Jeremy was in too much pain to go. He was terribly disappointed, but we were able to go on a trip with them the following week. The members were surprised and thrilled to see he had recovered so soon. They presented him with a "Get Well" card signed by all of them. They saw him as an intelligent and interesting boy, not as a troublesome one.

Busy summer ...

As soon as school ended in June, Jeremy started building a tree house in a stand of trees near the horse barn: boards, nails, power tools, roofing, and anything else he could think of, made a one-way trip to his new project. I didn't complain; the cost of nails and building supplies was a small price to pay to keep him busy and out of trouble. He was content and my possessions were safe.

Then the telephone was suddenly out of order. I called the phone company. A repairman came and checked the lines in the house.

"I can't find any problem with these lines. Do you have a phone somewhere else?"

"There's a phone out in the barn."

He followed me to the barn and I showed him the phone.

He pointed to a line that ran from the phone to the rafters. "What's that line?"

"I don't know," I said, but I knew . . . Jeremy.

The unfamiliar line connected to the phone box and continued through a vent in the side of the barn. We walked outside and looked at the wire strung between the barn and the tree house.

"What do you want me to do with that?" the repairman asked.

"Disconnect it."

A few minutes later, the line to the tree house was disconnected and my phone was operational. I promised the repairman it would not happen again.

I confronted Jeremy about the phone, "Do not do things without asking permission. Remember the 'P' word. Don't ever touch the phone lines again."

"Okaaaaaay!"

In July, I saw smoke rising from behind the barn. The weather had been very hot and dry; a burn ban was in effect. Jeremy built a fire next to some trees. I got the hose and put out the fire. It terrified me.

I kept matches locked in a safe, but he managed to acquire them somehow. It wasn't the first time he'd gotten matches somewhere. I'd often find burned Matchbox cars. He knew he wasn't supposed to start fires. He could have started a forest fire, destroyed our home and possibly caused injuries or death. It was a close call. I was afraid if he did it again, we wouldn't be so lucky. Another more serious discussion about the 'P' word was necessary. I hoped I convinced him how dangerous the consequences of this latest action were.

I signed him up in 4-H rabbits. Animals are good for kids and help them learn responsibility. He refused my help whenever I tried to instruct him do fitting and showing. He liked the rabbits, loved barn work and was enthusiastic at shows, but sitting quietly at meetings and getting along with the other kids was problematic.

Once again his lack of social skills got in the way. He was disruptive and ill-mannered. The other children from the ages of six to eighteen sat quietly and paid attention. Eleven-year-old Jeremy made noises, poked the other kids, and refused to behave and cooperate.

It was embarrassing and frustrating for me, but nothing I did put an end to his annoying habits. We participated for two years, but Jeremy did not make any significant progress in behavioral improvement during that time. The positive social developmental growth so apparent in other children associated with the program failed to materialize in my son.

Editor's Note:

Zenia remembers this stage in Jeremy's development as demonstrating that he could interact well with certain adults but continued to struggle with others. She tried to help him socialize with children his age. Her attempts generally failed. ODD children often have poorly developed social skills.

Middle School

Uncooperative as usual...

Most people lament about how much trouble their kids are as teenagers. I dreaded having to go through that, but one friend insisted that Jeremy was so bad at such an early age, he couldn't possibly get any worse. He was sure I would have a much easier time in the teenage years, and the worst would be behind me.

His former sixth grade teacher, who he liked, transferred to Jeremy's new middle school the same time twelve-year-old Jeremy entered seventh grade, and he was in her class. This school had a very unstructured, open learning center without walls between classrooms—not a good match for him.

Jeremy liked his knew school, at least for a while. He always did better when situations changed. As soon as things became familiar, he didn't like them anymore. Even though he liked this school for the time being, he still refused to do the majority of his homework or participate in classroom discussions or activities. Things deteriorated rapidly and he reverted to his normal uncooperative habits.

A boy stole his wallet, and Jeremy kicked the culprit to get his wallet back.

He was suspended from school.

When the principal called to explain, I was told, "He shouldn't have kicked the other boy; he should have just reported it."

"The other student stole, a criminal act," I said.

"We have to punish everyone the same."

"Perpetrators of crimes and victims receive the same punishment? That's ridiculous." I was dumbfounded.

After that phone conversation, I tried to explain to Jeremy that he had to report incidents to the principal or a teacher, not try to solve a situation himself.

"I just wanted to get my wallet back. He stole it!"

"Yes, but if anything happens again, make sure you tell your teacher or the principal."

"Okaaaay."

He was angry about the theft but happy to be suspended.

New home, new school...

I could no longer afford to keep my house. I sold the farm and bought ten wooded acres five miles away. We moved in with a friend, Gary, who lived in another county while our land was developed and a mobile home prepared. In February, thirteen-year-old Jeremy transferred to the new district and joined a new seventh grade class. We could no longer make the commute to his psychologist two counties away.

Gary, a merchant seaman, was at sea most of the time, so Jeremy and I were on our own. Jeremy's behavioral issues irritated Gary so much that he preferred staying away.

Middle school was a slight improvement over grade school. Once again, the new school was Jeremy's favorite school, but before long it was the worst. It was in a lower income district and didn't have all the benefits of schools in the county from which we'd moved. It was actually a fourth – eighth grade school and had none of the shop classes of a normal middle school. His teachers tried their best to work with him, and with me, but his lack of cooperation continued.

He did manage to do some homework under extreme duress, but he never could understand why it was required since he always did well on tests. Other students who turned in assignments didn't do as well on exams. Why do homework, Jeremy asked, if he could learn the material by being in school?

I don't know how his teachers tolerated reading his assignments. I'd seen him print neat letters, so I knew he could do it if he wanted to. Instead, his penmanship was deliberately atrocious and he was determined to keep it that way. He never left spaces between words and his handwriting was so illegible it was nearly impossible to decipher. His teachers refused to fail him in spite of failing grades. He knew the subject matter, and many teachers liked him.

He continued to be frequently suspended from the bus or from school. He didn't get along with other students on the bus and directed foul language at them and the driver. We lived less than a mile from this school, so he often walked home when he was suspended.

I received a number of calls from the school complaining that he was "running on the playground". Again, I had trouble with this philosophy. Running on the playground seemed like a good thing—a way for kids to burn off steam—particularly useful in Jeremy's case. The school was concerned about being sued if he ran into someone.

I had to tell him, "No running on the playground." Of course, there was no way for me to enforce it.

Teachers and counselors frequently phoned and requested appointments to see me. They always expected me to do something to alter his behavior. Of course, they never had any suggestions as to what that something might be. I'd been using the behavior modification method deemed best by psychologists—taking things away and having him earn them back. Success was minimal.

I tried giving him bread and water for dinner one night as punishment for his latest suspension off the bus for cursing at the driver and flipping her off.

Neither of us could recall the incident years later, but he'd obviously told someone. This was to be another case of "child abuse" come back to haunt me claiming my son would suffer from malnutrition from such treatment. My son ate ravenously his whole life. He never suffered in any way.

He still had problems getting along with other kids and got into a fight with a neighbor boy. He was no longer welcome in their home. There were a few other boys on our road his age, so he did manage to get to know some of them. He seldom brought friends home.

Relationship on shaky ground ...

My relationship with my friend, Gary, was on shaky ground. Jeremy was a continual source of aggravation for both of us as well as for the school system. No matter how well I got along with men in my private personal life, Jeremy always proved to be more of a challenge than they could tolerate. Gary couldn't stay out to sea all the time. He took vacations to visit friends in other states to escape.

Jeremy managed to irritate just about everyone. I made excuses for him, but it was hard on me. I loved my son and it was frustrating to have to keep defending him in spite of behaviors that were so unacceptable.

Why couldn't he behave in class and do his homework like other kids? Why did he have to screw up so many things? Why couldn't he follow rules? Social skills that were normal for others seemed to be impossible for Jeremy.

One male friend once told me Jeremy was evil—the devil. I didn't believe that, but I couldn't deny he did horrible things.

I noticed cars with bumper stickers stating, 'MY CHILD'S AN HONOR STUDENT.' I wondered what it would be like to raise such a child, but believed I'd never find out.

A nagging worry ...

I feared Jeremy would end up hurt, murdered, or spend his life in prison, all possible scenarios posed by psychologists who had been no more successful than I at altering his behavior. It was a nagging worry.

I let a friend, David, live in a motor home on my newly acquired acreage. During the summer, between seventh and eighth grade, Jeremy camped out there living in a tent. He got along well with David.

Jeremy was thrilled to be in the company of the men who drove the heavy diesel rigs. He wanted to learn how each one operated, and was thrilled when the excavator and backhoe drivers allowed him to drive their equipment and "help".

A man who cleared my land told me, "This isn't really work; it's fun. The excavator is a big toy." He was bored with retirement and bought a new excavator to get back to business and do my job. He encouraged my son, and Jeremy was thrilled with the opportunity.

The backhoe driver was equally indulging. Jeremy's love of heavy diesel equipment grew. He was in his element hanging out with men and their big rigs. It was an opportunity few boys could experience. Jeremy was disappointed when summer ended and he had to return to school.

Another Christmas...

We lived at Gary's house for one full year until our house was finally ready to move into. Problems at school continued. Gary was out to sea and Jeremy and I celebrated Christmas with Jim, a friend of Gary's who was staying at the house until he could catch a ship.

We had a very enjoyable holiday season. The electric company knocked down a nine foot tall fir tree when they installed the power line running to our future home. Jeremy didn't want to see the tree go to waste, so we brought it home. It was a rather odd-looking lopsided tree with a chopped-off top, not the prettiest Christmas tree.

We decorated it with ornaments, tinsel, and lit the lights. It didn't look bad with wrapped presents beneath it.

Jim, Jeremy and I spent time together baking and decorating cookies. Jim tolerated Jeremy better than Gary. Of course he didn't see Jeremy frequently.

Jeremy generally got along well with men as long as they weren't teachers or someone else expecting him to follow rules. Jeremy was sad when Jim went to sea in January. Of course he had to go back to school.

Wood Shop class...

In April, we moved into our "new home" and Jeremy transferred into another middle school. The new school had shop classes, something the previous school had not. Jeremy was put into wood shop in the middle of the semester. He loved and excelled in shop, and quickly caught up to and surpassed his fellow classmates. I had no trouble getting him up in the morning for a change. Wood shop was his first class.

I had a conference with his teacher. He told me, "You know what a wonderful son you have, and what a great student he is."

"No, I didn't know. This is the first time I've heard it. He hates school. He's always done terrible."

"Well, he's a terrific kid. He's doing a great job in my class."

I was flabbergasted. It felt wonderful to have a teacher actually compliment my son, an unexpected pleasure. A feeling I had never experienced.

Jeremy finished building an Adirondack chair. It still sits in my back yard.

Finally, something he liked...

The school counselor recommended Jeremy for a vocational technology school in the next county. As an eighth grader he could go for three weeks in the summer. Jeremy jumped at the chance. Finally, there was something about school he liked.

He signed up for auto repair and was very enthusiastic about his class. He got up every morning without any trouble, happy to go to summer school. It was amazing. All was not perfect, however. He had problems with another student in the class, and was expelled over the issue near the end of the term. I made him write a letter of apology to the school, and I took him to meet with the dean and counselor to apologize in person. I wanted to make sure he could go back next year.

The dean was very nice. She knew and liked Jeremy, and wanted him to come back. She was surprised a student would actually write an apology, or that a parent actually cared enough to bring him back to apologize. They'd be happy to have him return. The technical school was for kids who didn't fit in well in the standard school system, so they were very good with kids who had problems.

Jeremy spent his summer going around the area near our home and meeting people. He always seemed to find men who did car repair, welding or construction. He found someone clearing brush with a Bobcat. The driver allowed Jeremy to operate his machine. He hung out with loggers across the road and found odd jobs. We had a landscaper at the end of the road who also owned a Bobcat. He let Jeremy hang out and often gave him leftover job materials.

All in all, we had a good summer.

Editor's Note:

At this point, Jeremy is enjoying successful relationships with adult males who let him into their work or craftsmanship world. Zenia feels encouraged and grateful to these men. At the same time, Jeremy's behavior around her male friend, who assumed an authority role, was intolerable.

Jeremy's determination to do only what he wants to do, and to misbehave when he's not in control of his environment, discourages his mother, psychologist and teachers.

High school

Teenage years - vocational success, academic struggle...

Summer ended and another school year began. Jeremy entered high school, ninth grade. My friend's prophesy seemed to be coming true. Jeremy's behavior did seem to be improving as a teenager, now fourteen. I credit that to the positive male role models in his life.

He had a whole year of wood shop this time, another success story, another shop teacher who believed in him. This man told me numerous times how exceptional my son was. "He doesn't need plans; he can figure things out in his head. He made the most difficult project in the class."

I knew Jeremy's talent with building. He'd built a cabinet with doors on the lower part and open shelves on top. It sits in my dining room to this day.

"You don't need to worry about Jeremy," the shop teacher said. "He'll do well. It doesn't matter that he doesn't do well academically. School isn't practical for everyone. He'll be very successful. He can do construction or make custom furniture. He's a very talented woodworker. He'll have a good future and be able to earn a good living."

Those were encouraging words to hear, though I didn't totally agree. I believe academic achievement is important. Still, I was elated to hear such complimentary remarks regarding my son.

Other teachers and counselors had less positive things to say. An English teacher complained Jeremy refused to do any work in class, and since the teacher didn't send schoolwork home, that was not a good sign. A math teacher did send work home, but Jeremy consistently refused to turn it in.

If he did manage to get assignments home he still often refused to do them.

I tried another tack, making him sit on the floor with his assignments, paper and pencils, but he broke the pencils, and ate the paper. Getting him to do homework was no easier than it ever had been.

IEP (Individualized Education Program) ...

Counselors resubmitted IEP paperwork for Jeremy, and I listened to the expected problems with his scholastic performance and behavioral issues.

Jeremy hated being labeled as Special Ed, but even with counselors and teachers giving him extra help every year, he never seemed to get down to the business of doing assignments. His organizational skills were always deficient. Zip-up notebooks with special pockets and backpacks or briefcases didn't help. He continually lost his assignments or books. There were times when he actually finished assignments, but didn't bother to hand them in.

Another teacher complained he was causing problems in class, the same old issue of annoying other students; a difficult problem to overcome, and something totally out of my control.

High school students actually had to have enough credits at the end of four years to graduate. With failing grades in math and English, Jeremy would have to take those subjects again. He was angry.

I said, "If you'd done your homework you wouldn't have to take those classes again. That's your consequence."

"It's too boring. I want to be in a more advanced class."

"They won't put you in an advanced class until you do well in the basic class first. You have to prove you can do the work before they will let you advance."

"Tell them to put me in the advanced class. I can do the math."

"I'm sorry, but I can't do that. They wouldn't listen to me even if I did."

Summer school...

That summer Jeremy signed up for welding at summer school. He insisted he wanted to work with metal instead of wood. He loved the class, but it only lasted a few weeks. He spent the rest of the summer at a house being built at the end of our road.

He'd get up every morning at six and be over there waiting when the crew showed up. The framers had him pounding nails and cleaning up. He spent a lot of time working there and watching the builders. The framers even paid him several hundred dollars for his help that summer.

Metal shop ...

In tenth grade Jeremy registered for metal shop instead of wood shop. His shop teacher was the same man who'd taught him the year before. Because Jeremy had been so talented working with wood, his teacher tried to convince him to continue with that program, but, shortly after metal shop got under way, the teacher told me Jeremy's ability working with metal was equal to that of wood. He could earn a living easily in either field. The credits and A's grades he earned in shop class helped offset the low or failing grades plaguing his academic classes.

He took the state WASL (Washington Assessment of Student Learning) test, and failed the math and English sections. He was told they could watch a movie if they finished early, so he rushed through and suffered another consequence for his choice. He was to regret this the next year when he had to take a WASL prep class after school.

Jeremy loved wearing grungy clothes and considered it a "badge of honor" to wear the grime of labor so people would know he'd been working. He liked being a "blue-collar" worker. The school counselor called, concerned I didn't have money to wash his clothes. I was mortified. I explained he had plenty of clean clothes; he just refused to wear them, preferring to wear the dirty ones. It was still impossible to get him to do anything he didn't want to.

Every success with Jeremy was counterbalanced by his negative behaviors.

Forging a Friendship ...

Jeremy called me one Saturday evening and said he was at a friend's house a couple of miles down the road and he wanted to spend the night. The friend—a man owned a towing company complete with a junkyard. I spoke to his friend, Stan, on the phone and went over there to meet him. He had a wife and kids. Five acres of beat-up cars, all sizes of trucks, welders, huge garage with lifts and tools, lots of heavy equipment and mounds of stuff surrounded Stan's house. I could see the attraction for Jeremy.

Stan said he loved junk when he was a kid—it was fun to learn how to take things apart and fix engines. He said Jeremy needed a man to do things with. He liked Jeremy and enjoyed having him around. Jeremy didn't cause any trouble and could help out around the place.

I agreed to let Jeremy stay.

Stan put Jeremy to work. Jeremy was in heaven. I never had to wonder where he was. He'd hang out there doing odd jobs. He was more filthy than ever, but safe, staying out of trouble, and learning useful things.

Having a positive male role model changed his life.

At fifteen Jeremy was proficient at driving a forklift. Before he could take Driver's Ed, he learned to drive and maneuver big trucks on Stan's five acres. He learned how to hook up vehicles to be towed and rode with Stan or other drivers to help out.

When he got his learner's permit, I gave him driving lessons in my car. He was a pretty good driver. Experience with the forklift and moving vehicles around in the crowded junk yard had been good practice. I felt comfortable as a passenger when he was driving. His experience riding in the tow trucks and seeing the results of accidents firsthand instilled a sense of awareness and caution that carried over into his own driving.

He'd tell me about some of the things other kids did in Driver's Ed. He thought some of their inexperienced mistakes and fears were pretty funny.

Welding ...

Jeremy took welding in summer school and signed up for welding half-time his junior year. Students were allowed to spend half-time at the technical school the last two years of high school. I bought him a leather welder's jacket and helmet for his class.

He loved his summer of welding and working on cars at the junkyard. It was like pulling teeth to get him to help me at home, but I didn't have to worry about him getting into trouble. He finally had friends—other boys he'd met at the tech school. They were good kids, who didn't drink or do drugs. They spent all their time working on cars.

That year he took metal shop again with a new teacher who started a Robot Bot-Ball group that met after school. They were going to compete in a competition in California in the spring. Jeremy joined the group, excited about robots.

He got upset when he had to miss some "robot time" to go to WASL prep classes for students who'd barely failed the exam.

"I don't need those classes," he argued. "They don't make the kids who failed badly take them."

I checked into that to verify what he was telling me, and learned that only marginal students qualified for the prep class. Students who did poorly had to take the whole subject over. He failed by a slim margin, so could get by taking the prep class.

Jeremy said, "I'll pass next time, I won't rush through like last time."

"Well, you should have tried harder the first time. This is your consequence for rushing, and you can't graduate if you don't pass. It's important to do well."

He went to the classes, but he wasn't happy about it. He did pass the WASL.

Robots and team work ...

The kids doing Bot-Ball were a mixed bag who didn't work well as a team. None of them competed in sports, so they weren't team oriented by experience. They got off to a rocky start, but they had a great trip to California even though their robot came in almost last. Most of the other groups had competed for years and their teachers were very experienced.

They did well for a first year team, and were proud of their effort. The local newspaper published an article about their trip with a photo of them.

Jeremy started a Young Republicans Club at school and was their first president. The Democrats had a club for years. The conservative point of view had been unrepresented until Jeremy took a stand. He persistently fought for his political party. He set up a political talk show via the internet on his computer.

Again, Jeremy worked hard on projects that interested him.

Driving accident ...

Jeremy caused a car accident in my pickup truck while on his way back from picking up our lawnmower from the repair shop. He saw a woman with a flat tire on the other side of the highway and decided to help, a nice gesture, but an accident resulted when he made a left turn in front of an oncoming SUV. He was lucky he was in my 3/4 ton truck instead of a small car. He wasn't hurt, but it was too far from Stan's wrecking yard, so another towing company had to be called. I expected Jeremy to pay the fees and the purchase price of a truck a friend offered to sell me.

My wrecked truck became one of Jeremy's projects.

Glass art ...

Senior year, Jeremy assisted the welding class as teacher's aide, registered for glass-art, and signed up for Navy Reserve. As he wasn't yet eighteen, I went with him to the recruiting center to give written consent. He couldn't actually enlist until he graduated.

I tried to convince the recruiter Jeremy wasn't good military material; he refused to follow rules or do anything he was told. The recruiter told me those kids often do surprisingly well. I was quite dubious, unable to believe that Jeremy would be successful in the military. He was to prove me wrong.

Jeremy decided to actively enlist in September, after summer vacation. Now he had more incentive to finish school. I ordered his cap and gown, elated he was actually going to graduate.

A few weeks before the end of the semester, I received the familiar notices; he was missing assignments in a political science class and several art projects and wasn't going to graduate if they weren't done.

"Why haven't you turned in your art projects? You love art. Get them done! The Navy won't take you if you don't graduate!"

He completed his art projects and earned an A, turning in some outstanding, beautiful works of art. He brought home a frosted glass picture of a buck in a forest, created from a picture he'd found online. He crafted a skull with stained glass. The soldering was solid and perfect, a much better job than I could ever have made, and I'd worked extensively with stained glass. He demonstrated exceptional talent.

I praised his work for the craftsmanship and asked if all the students did such complex projects.

"Nah, most of them did really lame ones."

"Why didn't you do these sooner?"

"I don't know."

Graduation his way ...

Jeremy signed up for machine shop for summer school.

"How can you sign up for summer school?" I asked. You'll be a graduate. You won't qualify for tech school."

"Yeah, I just can."

I was becoming suspicious. As school drew to a close, he admitted he was short half a credit for not finishing his political science assignments.

So ended my hope of seeing Jeremy in a cap and gown, graduating with his class. Though I had told family members the graduation date, I hadn't sent invitations.

They weren't surprised. At least we were getting closer. The Navy was on his back. He was motivated to complete his credits and get his diploma, albeit late.

Jeremy had one more struggle to complete his high school education. He went to summer school every day, but his report card got lost in the mail, delaying his accreditation and eligibility for Navy Reserve.

He spent the rest of the summer working for pay, and fit in a few chores he'd promised to do for me. Getting him to work for me was never easy. Unfortunately, he didn't finish rebuilding my truck before leaving for Navy Reserve training duty.

Editor's Note:

Zenia points out two important factors in Jeremy's development; he clings to his determination to do things his way, and he thrives with appropriate adult male role models.

Adulthood

Navy success...

Jeremy headed for Great Lakes Navy base in Illinois in the middle of September. I got a quick phone call when he got there, then didn't hear from him again until he graduated from basic training in November.

Jeremy graduated second in his class, and his class scored second highest overall. Michael flew back there for the event.

From Illinois, Jeremy flew to Los Angeles where he was driven to Port Heuneme, California, for mechanic training with the Navy Sea Bees. Again, he graduated near the top of his class.

My disorganized, grungy son came home wearing a uniform, full of ideas and grand plans of all he was going to get done. He continued working on trucks, but one weekend a month, he got cleaned up, put on a uniform, and went off for Reserve duty.

At age nineteen, he used his wages from the military to establish a mobile welding and automotive repair company. He remained active in the Navy Reserve.

He did a tour of duty in Afghanistan the next year and called home almost every week while he was there.

Once back home, he removed most of his accumulation of truck and car parts from my property.

He went back to work for Stan, driving a tow truck this time, and did other odd jobs at the tow yard. Several months later, another towing company offered him a better paying job. Jeremy hired on for six months, working seven days a week.

When he turned twenty-one, he enrolled in the Universal Technical Institute in Sacramento, California, to become a certified diesel mechanic.

He finished six weeks ahead of the rest of his class, graduating near the top and returning home with a fiancée.

He's currently successfully employed as a diesel mechanic, is still in the U.S. Navy Reserves and expects to do more active duty. He has been promoted several times and is now a 2nd class petty officer E5.

He seems to be a workaholic who enjoys his job. He has come a long way and has already achieved far more than I ever dared to hope.

I am proud of my successful, patriotic son.

Looking Back

Jeremy cannot explain why he behaved as he did or identify any reason for his anger. When teachers and professionals threw up their hands and said they could do no more with him, I continued encouraging him, reminding him about rules and the consequences of ignoring them.

He's a very talented artist, which I encouraged. While each of the artistic endeavors held his interest for a time, none became a center of focus.

The men who took an interest in him in shop classes recognized and encouraged his drive. His creative energy took off and blossomed. Pride in his accomplishments fueled his ambition and he was on the road to excellence.

He was not a throw-away child as some people insinuated. While his transformation was excruciatingly slow, especially in the early years, it manifested in useful life-altering directions.

It is important to remember this did not carry over in other areas of his life and school. His miserable scholastic record continued throughout school until he went into the military. Only then did he turn things around and accept the importance of doing what was expected of him and follow through. Determination to be successful in diesel mechanic school drove him to excel.

Throughout his younger life, he never doubted his abilities. Just the opposite, he was determined to do whatever he set out to do. This was evident in our constant battle over asking for permission—the "P" word. He'd find something that he figured he could fix, improve, or take for his use.

He highly overrated his skills and abilities and destroyed many devices. That self-confidence, once the bane of my existence, has been useful in his career. He has never shied from looking for work and has been extremely successful in procuring and holding down jobs.

It was a tremendous relief when I could actually stop fearing what was going to happen to him. Taking pride in his success has been my greatest pleasure.

While he's succeeding, I've had a personal struggle that dates back to the two incidents in his childhood when I followed friends' suggestions to change Jeremy's behaviors. In both cases, I told the professional psychologist what I'd done.

After several years of working with elderly clients as an adult caregiver, I lost my position due to a "failed background check." Those incidents were recorded in Child Protective Services reports as a "Finding of Abuse." They came up when adult caregiver services began checking CPS reports.

In spite of being considered a compassionate caregiver by my employer and well-liked by my clients, I am unable to continue in that work without legal intervention to remove the finding.

End Notes

Zenia says...

Rearing a child with behavioral problems is extremely difficult under the best of circumstances. Disciplinary actions that work for normal children are often unsuccessful with Oppositional Defiant Disorder children. Trying to get them to conform to a "one size fits all" disciplinary system is ineffectual, impractical, and does a disservice to their teachers and counselors.

Children who are hyperactive need ways to channel their energy. Their needs often conflict with a school's safety rules.

Parents who struggle to rear difficult children are often criticized and humiliated by the general populace who don't understand the child's disorder. Parents suffer from frustration, depression and extreme feelings of guilt. They are misjudged and blamed for having poor parenting skills, being abusive, or worse. They become isolated, which exacerbates their exhaustion and depression.

In the wake of mass shootings punctuated by the massacres at the theater in Aurora, Colorado, and Sandy Hook School in Newtown, Connecticut, our country is looking at control measures and, to a lesser extent, mental health issues. How should society address and treat mental health issues in children?

I fear this is an issue that will not be resolved easily or soon. My son needed positive male role models long before he found them on his own. I needed understanding and support for my role as his mother in a rural community with limited resources for children diagnosed with serious problems.

I would like to see an education system in this country where children who struggle academically while showing interest and success in vocational areas could be channeled into hands-on programs. Other countries have done that for students with needs and interests similar to Jeremy's.

Finding an alternative choice and encouraged by the men who taught him made all the difference for my son. As a single mother raising a unique, challenged boy I have a great appreciation for these special men.

These children all possess positive attributes. They have likes and dislikes and definite fields of interest. Rather than trying to force them to conform to a system that doesn't work for them, it is important to encourage them to develop the talents they have in directions that motivate them.

Parents need to be aided in this lonely, difficult obligation rather then left to struggle on their own. Strong-willed children can become outstanding citizens. Independent determination when focused in a positive direction can lead these children to productive and happy lives.

To Jeremy, from Zenia ...

Meant to Be

I held you in my arms, a beautiful, perfect baby,
Expectations for your future, in my head already.

Before I knew it, you were walking; I'd catch you when you'd fall,
You were off and running, in what seemed no time at all.

The first day of school, you turned and waved goodbye.
I watched you go and wiped a tear from my eye.

Teachers were confounded, frustrated, aggravated.
They tried every way they could to get you motivated.

Rules were never meant for you.
There was nothing we could do.

Your future seemed in jeopardy.
You rebelled at every opportunity.

A creative, inquisitive, ingenious mind,
School had you feeling too confined.

In shop class you displayed your ability,
Wowing teachers with diligence and ingenuity.

Sparks flying, welding, shaping metal,
Or beneath a truck covered in grease or diesel.

Your choice of career, I would not have selected.
What's right for you, I've finally accepted.

Staunch, conservative, political activist,
Outgoing, charismatic conversationalist

You march to the beat of a different drum.
Responsible, honorable man you've become.

I have no doubt of your success,
With all the qualities you possess.

I send you into the world on your own.
I couldn't be prouder of you, my son.

You followed a path I hadn't foreseen.
But you are who you were meant to be.

Editor's Note:

An online review of the literature on Oppositional Defiant Disorder will provide readers with information on diagnoses, symptoms, causes and suggested treatment. The following is a brief list of resources. Each of them will lead you to additional information.

DSM-IV & DSM-IV TR (BehaveNet)
www.behavenet.com/cappsules/disorders/odd.htm

American Family Physician – Oppositional Defiant Disorder
www.aafp.org/afp

Oppositional Defiant Disorder (ODD)
www.mayoclinic.com/health/oppositional-defiant-disorder/DS

http://addadhdadvances.com/ODD.html

CPSIA information can be obtained at www.ICGtesting.com
Printed in the USA
LVOW07s1512031014

407163LV00001B/219/P